ENCOU
SCRIPTURES

GRATITUDE
JOURNAL
FOR MEN
OF FAITH

THIS JOURNAL BELONGS TO:

_____

DATE:

_____

If found, please return to:

Address: _____
_____
Phone: _____
Email: _____

M T W Th F Sat Sun _____/_____/_____

TODAY I'M GRATEFUL FOR:

_____

_____

_____

_____

_____

MY PRAYER FOR TODAY:

_____

_____

_____

_____

_____

_____

For God so loved the world, that he gave his only begotten Son,
that whosoever believeth in him should not perish,
but have everlasting life. — John 3:16 (KJV)

M T W Th F Sat Sun _____/_____/_____

TODAY I'M GRATEFUL FOR:

_____

_____

_____

_____

MY PRAYER FOR TODAY:

_____

_____

_____

_____

_____

M T W Th F Sat Sun _____/_____/_____

TODAY I'M GRATEFUL FOR:

_____

_____

_____

_____

_____

MY PRAYER FOR TODAY:

_____

_____

_____

_____

_____

And we know that all things work together for good to them that love God, to them who are the called according to his purpose. — Romans 8:28 (KJV)

M T W Th F Sat Sun _____/_____/_____

TODAY I'M GRATEFUL FOR:

_____

_____

_____

_____

MY PRAYER FOR TODAY:

_____

_____

_____

_____

_____

M T W Th F Sat Sun _____/_____/_____

TODAY I'M GRATEFUL FOR:

_____
_____
_____
_____

MY PRAYER FOR TODAY:

_____
_____
_____
_____
_____

I can do all things through Christ which strengtheneth me. — Philippians 4:13 (KJV)

M T W Th F Sat Sun _____/_____/_____

TODAY I'M GRATEFUL FOR:

_____
_____
_____
_____

MY PRAYER FOR TODAY:

_____
_____
_____
_____
_____

M T W Th F Sat Sun _____ / _____ / _____

TODAY I'M GRATEFUL FOR:

_____
_____
_____
_____

MY PRAYER FOR TODAY:

_____
_____
_____
_____
_____

Trust in the Lord with all thine heart; and lean not unto thine own understanding. In all thy ways acknowledge him, and he shall direct thy paths. — Proverbs 3:5-6 (KJV)

M T W Th F Sat Sun _____ / _____ / _____

TODAY I'M GRATEFUL FOR:

_____
_____
_____
_____

MY PRAYER FOR TODAY:

_____
_____
_____
_____
_____

M T W Th F Sat Sun _____ / _____ / _____

TODAY I'M GRATEFUL FOR:

_____
_____
_____
_____

MY PRAYER FOR TODAY:

_____
_____
_____
_____
_____

For by grace are ye saved through faith; and that not of yourselves: it is the gift of God: Not of works, lest any man should boast. — Ephesians 2:8-9 (KJV)

M T W Th F Sat Sun _____ / _____ / _____

TODAY I'M GRATEFUL FOR:

_____
_____
_____
_____

MY PRAYER FOR TODAY:

_____
_____
_____
_____
_____

M T W Th F Sat Sun _____ / _____ / _____

TODAY I'M GRATEFUL FOR:

_____
_____
_____
_____

MY PRAYER FOR TODAY:

_____
_____
_____
_____
_____

And be not conformed to this world: but be ye transformed by the renewing of your mind, that ye may prove what is that good, and acceptable, and perfect, will of God. — Romans 12:2 (KJV)

M T W Th F Sat Sun _____ / _____ / _____

TODAY I'M GRATEFUL FOR:

_____
_____
_____
_____

MY PRAYER FOR TODAY:

_____
_____
_____
_____
_____

M T W Th F Sat Sun _____/_____/_____

TODAY I'M GRATEFUL FOR:

_____
_____
_____
_____
_____

MY PRAYER FOR TODAY:

_____
_____
_____
_____
_____
_____

Be careful for nothing; but in every thing by prayer and supplication with thanksgiving let your requests be made known unto God. — Philipians 4:6 (KJV)

M T W Th F Sat Sun _____/_____/_____

TODAY I'M GRATEFUL FOR:

_____
_____
_____
_____
_____

MY PRAYER FOR TODAY:

_____
_____
_____
_____
_____
_____

M T W Th F Sat Sun _____ / _____ / _____

TODAY I'M GRATEFUL FOR:

_____
_____
_____
_____
_____

MY PRAYER FOR TODAY:

_____
_____
_____
_____
_____

> But the fruit of the Spirit is love, joy, peace, longsuffering, gentleness, goodness, faith, meekness, temperance: against such there is no law. — Galatians 5:22-23 (KJV)

M T W Th F Sat Sun _____ / _____ / _____

TODAY I'M GRATEFUL FOR:

_____
_____
_____
_____

MY PRAYER FOR TODAY:

_____
_____
_____
_____
_____

M T W Th F Sat Sun _____ / _____ / _____

TODAY I'M GRATEFUL FOR:

_____
_____
_____
_____
_____

MY PRAYER FOR TODAY:

_____
_____
_____
_____
_____

> I beseech you therefore, brethren, by the mercies of God, that ye present your bodies a living sacrifice, holy, acceptable unto God, which is your reasonable service. — Romans 12:1 (KJV)

M T W Th F Sat Sun _____ / _____ / _____

TODAY I'M GRATEFUL FOR:

_____
_____
_____
_____

MY PRAYER FOR TODAY:

_____
_____
_____
_____
_____

M T W Th F Sat Sun _____/_____/_____

TODAY I'M GRATEFUL FOR:

_____
_____
_____
_____

MY PRAYER FOR TODAY:

_____
_____
_____
_____
_____

The thief cometh not, but for to steal, and to kill, and to destroy:
I am come that they might have life, and that they might have
it more abundantly. — John 10:10 (KJV)

M T W Th F Sat Sun _____/_____/_____

TODAY I'M GRATEFUL FOR:

_____
_____
_____
_____

MY PRAYER FOR TODAY:

_____
_____
_____
_____
_____

M T W Th F Sat Sun _____/_____/_____

TODAY I'M GRATEFUL FOR:

_____
_____
_____
_____
_____

MY PRAYER FOR TODAY:

_____
_____
_____
_____
_____

If we confess our sins, he is faithful and just to forgive us our sins, and to cleanse us from all unrighteousness. — 1 John 1:9 (KJV)

M T W Th F Sat Sun _____/_____/_____

TODAY I'M GRATEFUL FOR:

_____
_____
_____
_____
_____

MY PRAYER FOR TODAY:

_____
_____
_____
_____
_____

M T W Th F Sat Sun _____/_____/_____

TODAY I'M GRATEFUL FOR:

_____
_____
_____
_____

MY PRAYER FOR TODAY:

_____
_____
_____
_____
_____

Jesus saith unto him, I am the way, the truth, and the life:
no man cometh unto the Father, but by me. — John 14:6 (KJV)

M T W Th F Sat Sun _____/_____/_____

TODAY I'M GRATEFUL FOR:

_____
_____
_____
_____

MY PRAYER FOR TODAY:

_____
_____
_____
_____
_____

M T W Th F Sat Sun _____ / _____ / _____

TODAY I'M GRATEFUL FOR:

_____

_____

_____

_____

MY PRAYER FOR TODAY:

_____

_____

_____

_____

_____

But God commendeth his love toward us, in that, while we were yet sinners, Christ died for us. — Romans 5:8 (KJV)

M T W Th F Sat Sun _____ / _____ / _____

TODAY I'M GRATEFUL FOR:

_____

_____

_____

_____

MY PRAYER FOR TODAY:

_____

_____

_____

_____

_____

M T W Th F Sat Sun _____ / _____ / _____

TODAY I'M GRATEFUL FOR:

_____
_____
_____
_____
_____

MY PRAYER FOR TODAY:

_____
_____
_____
_____
_____

For the wages of sin is death; but the gift of God is eternal life through Jesus Christ our Lord. — Romans 6:23 (KJV)

M T W Th F Sat Sun _____ / _____ / _____

TODAY I'M GRATEFUL FOR:

_____
_____
_____
_____
_____

MY PRAYER FOR TODAY:

_____
_____
_____
_____
_____

M T W Th F Sat Sun _____/_____/_____

TODAY I'M GRATEFUL FOR:

_____
_____
_____
_____

MY PRAYER FOR TODAY:

_____
_____
_____
_____
_____

But he was wounded for our transgressions, he was bruised for our iniquities: the chastisement of our peace was upon him; and with his stripes we are healed. — Isaiah 53:5 (KJV)

M T W Th F Sat Sun _____/_____/_____

TODAY I'M GRATEFUL FOR:

_____
_____
_____
_____

MY PRAYER FOR TODAY:

_____
_____
_____
_____
_____

M T W Th F Sat Sun _____/_____/_____

TODAY I'M GRATEFUL FOR:

_____
_____
_____
_____

MY PRAYER FOR TODAY:

_____
_____
_____
_____
_____

And the peace of God, which passeth all understanding,
shall keep your hearts and minds through Christ Jesus.
— Philippians 4:7 (KJV)

M T W Th F Sat Sun _____/_____/_____

TODAY I'M GRATEFUL FOR:

_____
_____
_____
_____

MY PRAYER FOR TODAY:

_____
_____
_____
_____
_____

M T W Th F Sat Sun _____/_____/_____

TODAY I'M GRATEFUL FOR:

_____
_____
_____
_____
_____

MY PRAYER FOR TODAY:

_____
_____
_____
_____
_____

Have not I commanded thee? Be strong and of a good courage;
be not afraid, neither be thou dismayed: for the Lord thy God is with
thee whithersoever thou goest. — Joshua 1:9 (KJV)

M T W Th F Sat Sun _____/_____/_____

TODAY I'M GRATEFUL FOR:

_____
_____
_____
_____

MY PRAYER FOR TODAY:

_____
_____
_____
_____
_____

M T W Th F Sat Sun _____ / _____ / _____

TODAY I'M GRATEFUL FOR:

_____
_____
_____
_____

MY PRAYER FOR TODAY:

_____
_____
_____
_____
_____

But they that wait upon the Lord shall renew their strength; they shall mount up with wings as eagles; they shall run, and not be weary; and they shall walk, and not faint. — Isaiah 40:31 (KJV)

M T W Th F Sat Sun _____ / _____ / _____

TODAY I'M GRATEFUL FOR:

_____
_____
_____
_____

MY PRAYER FOR TODAY:

_____
_____
_____
_____

M T W Th F Sat Sun _____/_____/_____

TODAY I'M GRATEFUL FOR:

_____
_____
_____
_____

MY PRAYER FOR TODAY:

_____
_____
_____
_____
_____

For by grace are ye saved through faith; and that not of yourselves: it is the gift of God: Not of works, lest any man should boast. — Ephesians 2:8-9 (KJV)

M T W Th F Sat Sun _____/_____/_____

TODAY I'M GRATEFUL FOR:

_____
_____
_____
_____

MY PRAYER FOR TODAY:

_____
_____
_____
_____
_____

M T W Th F Sat Sun _____/_____/_____

TODAY I'M GRATEFUL FOR:

_____
_____
_____
_____
_____

MY PRAYER FOR TODAY:

_____
_____
_____
_____
_____
_____

For the wages of sin is death; but the gift of God is eternal life
through Jesus Christ our Lord. — Romans 6:23 (KJV)

M T W Th F Sat Sun _____/_____/_____

TODAY I'M GRATEFUL FOR:

_____
_____
_____
_____
_____

MY PRAYER FOR TODAY:

_____
_____
_____
_____
_____
_____

M T W Th F Sat Sun _____/_____/_____

TODAY I'M GRATEFUL FOR:

_____
_____
_____
_____

MY PRAYER FOR TODAY:

_____
_____
_____
_____
_____

But seek ye first the kingdom of God, and his righteousness;
and all these things shall be added unto you. — Matthew 6:33 (KJV)

M T W Th F Sat Sun _____/_____/_____

TODAY I'M GRATEFUL FOR:

_____
_____
_____
_____

MY PRAYER FOR TODAY:

_____
_____
_____
_____
_____

M T W Th F Sat Sun _____/_____/_____

TODAY I'M GRATEFUL FOR:

_____

_____

_____

_____

MY PRAYER FOR TODAY:

_____

_____

_____

_____

_____

Humble yourselves therefore under the mighty hand of God, that he may exalt you in due time: casting all your care upon him; for he careth for you. — 1 Peter 5:6-7 (KJV)

M T W Th F Sat Sun _____/_____/_____

TODAY I'M GRATEFUL FOR:

_____

_____

_____

_____

MY PRAYER FOR TODAY:

_____

_____

_____

_____

_____

M T W Th F Sat Sun _____/_____/_____

TODAY I'M GRATEFUL FOR:

_____
_____
_____
_____

MY PRAYER FOR TODAY:

_____
_____
_____
_____
_____

For we are his workmanship, created in Christ Jesus unto good works, which God hath before ordained that we should walk in them. — Ephesians 2:10 (KJV)

M T W Th F Sat Sun _____/_____/_____

TODAY I'M GRATEFUL FOR:

_____
_____
_____
_____

MY PRAYER FOR TODAY:

_____
_____
_____
_____
_____

M T W Th F Sat Sun _____/_____/_____

TODAY I'M GRATEFUL FOR:

_____
_____
_____
_____

MY PRAYER FOR TODAY:

_____
_____
_____
_____
_____

Come unto me, all ye that labour and are heavy laden,
and I will give you rest. — Matthew 11:28 (KJV)

M T W Th F Sat Sun _____/_____/_____

TODAY I'M GRATEFUL FOR:

_____
_____
_____
_____

MY PRAYER FOR TODAY:

_____
_____
_____
_____
_____

M T W Th F Sat Sun _____/_____/_____

TODAY I'M GRATEFUL FOR:

_____
_____
_____
_____

MY PRAYER FOR TODAY:

_____
_____
_____
_____
_____

**Now faith is the substance of things hoped for,
the evidence of things not seen. — Hebrews 11:1 (KJV)**

M T W Th F Sat Sun _____/_____/_____

TODAY I'M GRATEFUL FOR:

_____
_____
_____
_____

MY PRAYER FOR TODAY:

_____
_____
_____
_____

M T W Th F Sat Sun _____ / _____ / _____

TODAY I'M GRATEFUL FOR:

MY PRAYER FOR TODAY:

Fear thou not; for I am with thee: be not dismayed; for I am thy God:
I will strengthen thee; yea, I will help thee; yea, I will uphold thee
with the right hand of my righteousness. — Isaiah 41:10 (KJV)

M T W Th F Sat Sun _____ / _____ / _____

TODAY I'M GRATEFUL FOR:

MY PRAYER FOR TODAY:

M T W Th F Sat Sun _____/_____/_____

TODAY I'M GRATEFUL FOR:

_____
_____
_____
_____
_____

MY PRAYER FOR TODAY:

_____
_____
_____
_____
_____

Take my yoke upon you, and learn of me; for I am meek and lowly in heart: and ye shall find rest unto your souls. — Matthew 11:29 (KJV)

M T W Th F Sat Sun _____/_____/_____

TODAY I'M GRATEFUL FOR:

_____
_____
_____
_____
_____

MY PRAYER FOR TODAY:

_____
_____
_____
_____
_____

M T W Th F Sat Sun _____/_____/_____

TODAY I'M GRATEFUL FOR:

_____
_____
_____
_____

MY PRAYER FOR TODAY:

_____
_____
_____
_____
_____

These things I have spoken unto you, that in me ye might
have peace. In the world ye shall have tribulation: but be of good
cheer; I have overcome the world. — John 16:33 (KJV)

M T W Th F Sat Sun _____/_____/_____

TODAY I'M GRATEFUL FOR:

_____
_____
_____
_____

MY PRAYER FOR TODAY:

_____
_____
_____
_____
_____

M T W Th F Sat Sun _____/_____/_____

TODAY I'M GRATEFUL FOR:

_____
_____
_____
_____

MY PRAYER FOR TODAY:

_____
_____
_____
_____
_____

For God hath not given us the spirit of fear; but of power, and of love, and of a sound mind. — 2 Timothy 1:7 (KJV)

M T W Th F Sat Sun _____/_____/_____

TODAY I'M GRATEFUL FOR:

_____
_____
_____
_____

MY PRAYER FOR TODAY:

_____
_____
_____
_____
_____

M T W Th F Sat Sun _____ / _____ / _____

TODAY I'M GRATEFUL FOR:

_____
_____
_____
_____

MY PRAYER FOR TODAY:

_____
_____
_____
_____
_____

Now the God of hope fill you with all joy and peace in believing, that ye may abound in hope, through the power of the Holy Ghost. — Romans 15:13 (KJV)

M T W Th F Sat Sun _____ / _____ / _____

TODAY I'M GRATEFUL FOR:

_____
_____
_____
_____

MY PRAYER FOR TODAY:

_____
_____
_____
_____
_____

M T W Th F Sat Sun _____/_____/_____

TODAY I'M GRATEFUL FOR:

_____
_____
_____
_____

MY PRAYER FOR TODAY:

_____
_____
_____
_____
_____

I am the resurrection, and the life: he that believeth in me, though he were dead, yet shall he live: And whosoever liveth and believeth in me shall never die. — John 11:25-26 (KJV)

M T W Th F Sat Sun _____/_____/_____

TODAY I'M GRATEFUL FOR:

_____
_____
_____
_____

MY PRAYER FOR TODAY:

_____
_____
_____
_____
_____

M T W Th F Sat Sun _____/_____/_____

TODAY I'M GRATEFUL FOR:

_____
_____
_____
_____

MY PRAYER FOR TODAY:

_____
_____
_____
_____
_____

Rest in the Lord, and wait patiently for him: fret not thyself because of him who prospereth in his way, because of the man who bringeth wicked devices to pass. — Psalm 37:7 (KJV)

M T W Th F Sat Sun _____/_____/_____

TODAY I'M GRATEFUL FOR:

_____
_____
_____
_____

MY PRAYER FOR TODAY:

_____
_____
_____
_____
_____

M T W Th F Sat Sun _____ / _____ / _____

TODAY I'M GRATEFUL FOR:

_____
_____
_____
_____

MY PRAYER FOR TODAY:

_____
_____
_____
_____
_____

He that heareth my word, and believeth on him that sent me, hath everlasting life, and shall not come into condemnation; but is passed from death unto life. — John 5:24 (KJV)

M T W Th F Sat Sun _____ / _____ / _____

TODAY I'M GRATEFUL FOR:

_____
_____
_____
_____

MY PRAYER FOR TODAY:

_____
_____
_____
_____
_____

M T W Th F Sat Sun _____ / _____ / _____

TODAY I'M GRATEFUL FOR:

_____
_____
_____
_____

MY PRAYER FOR TODAY:

_____
_____
_____
_____
_____

Consider it a great joy, my brothers and sisters, whenever you experience various trials, because you know that the testing of your faith produces endurance. — James 1:2-3 (CSB)

M T W Th F Sat Sun _____ / _____ / _____

TODAY I'M GRATEFUL FOR:

_____
_____
_____
_____

MY PRAYER FOR TODAY:

_____
_____
_____
_____
_____

M T W Th F Sat Sun _____/_____/_____

TODAY I'M GRATEFUL FOR:

_____
_____
_____
_____
_____

MY PRAYER FOR TODAY:

_____
_____
_____
_____
_____
_____

Repent, and be baptized every one of you in the name
of Jesus Christ for the remission of sins, and ye shall receive
the gift of the Holy Ghost. —Acts 2:38 (KJV)

M T W Th F Sat Sun _____/_____/_____

TODAY I'M GRATEFUL FOR:

_____
_____
_____
_____

MY PRAYER FOR TODAY:

_____
_____
_____
_____
_____

M T W Th F Sat Sun _____ / _____ / _____

TODAY I'M GRATEFUL FOR:

_____
_____
_____
_____

MY PRAYER FOR TODAY:

_____
_____
_____
_____
_____

And let the peace of God rule in your hearts, to the
which also ye are called in one body; and be
ye thankful. — Colossians 3:15 (KJV)

M T W Th F Sat Sun _____ / _____ / _____

TODAY I'M GRATEFUL FOR:

_____
_____
_____
_____

MY PRAYER FOR TODAY:

_____
_____
_____
_____
_____

M T W Th F Sat Sun _____/_____/_____

TODAY I'M GRATEFUL FOR:

_____
_____
_____
_____

MY PRAYER FOR TODAY:

_____
_____
_____
_____
_____

> Confess your faults one to another, and pray one for another, that ye may be healed. The effectual fervent prayer of a righteous man availeth much. — James 5:16 (KJV)

M T W Th F Sat Sun _____/_____/_____

TODAY I'M GRATEFUL FOR:

_____
_____
_____
_____

MY PRAYER FOR TODAY:

_____
_____
_____
_____
_____

M T W Th F Sat Sun _____/_____/_____

TODAY I'M GRATEFUL FOR:

_____
_____
_____
_____

MY PRAYER FOR TODAY:

_____
_____
_____
_____
_____

But my God shall supply all your need according to his riches in glory by Christ Jesus. — Philippians 4:19 (KJV)

M T W Th F Sat Sun _____/_____/_____

TODAY I'M GRATEFUL FOR:

_____
_____
_____
_____

MY PRAYER FOR TODAY:

_____
_____
_____
_____

M T W Th F Sat Sun _____/_____/_____

TODAY I'M GRATEFUL FOR:

_____
_____
_____
_____

MY PRAYER FOR TODAY:

_____
_____
_____
_____
_____

In the beginning was the Word, and the Word was with God, and the Word was God. — John 1:1 (KJV)

M T W Th F Sat Sun _____/_____/_____

TODAY I'M GRATEFUL FOR:

_____
_____
_____
_____

MY PRAYER FOR TODAY:

_____
_____
_____
_____
_____

M T W Th F Sat Sun _____ / _____ / _____

TODAY I'M GRATEFUL FOR:

_____
_____
_____
_____
_____

MY PRAYER FOR TODAY:

_____
_____
_____
_____
_____
_____

"For I know the plans I have for you," declares the Lord, "plans to prosper you and not to harm you, plans to give you hope and a future." — Jeremiah 29:11 (NIV)

M T W Th F Sat Sun _____ / _____ / _____

TODAY I'M GRATEFUL FOR:

_____
_____
_____
_____

MY PRAYER FOR TODAY:

_____
_____
_____
_____
_____

M T W Th F Sat Sun _____ / _____ / _____

TODAY I'M GRATEFUL FOR:

_____
_____
_____
_____

MY PRAYER FOR TODAY:

_____
_____
_____
_____
_____

Peace I leave with you, my peace I give unto you: not as the world giveth, give I unto you. Let not your heart be troubled, neither let it be afraid. — John 14:27 (KJV)

M T W Th F Sat Sun _____ / _____ / _____

TODAY I'M GRATEFUL FOR:

_____
_____
_____
_____

MY PRAYER FOR TODAY:

_____
_____
_____
_____
_____

M T W Th F Sat Sun _____ / _____ / _____

TODAY I'M GRATEFUL FOR:

_____
_____
_____
_____

MY PRAYER FOR TODAY:

_____
_____
_____
_____
_____

He hath shewed thee, O man, what is good; and what doth the Lord require of thee, but to do justly, and to love mercy, and to walk humbly with thy God? —Micah 6:8 (KJV)

M T W Th F Sat Sun _____ / _____ / _____

TODAY I'M GRATEFUL FOR:

_____
_____
_____
_____

MY PRAYER FOR TODAY:

_____
_____
_____
_____

M T W Th F Sat Sun _____/_____/_____

TODAY I'M GRATEFUL FOR:

_____
_____
_____
_____
_____

MY PRAYER FOR TODAY:

_____
_____
_____
_____
_____
_____

Greater love hath no man than this, that a man lay down his life for his friends. — John 15:13 (KJV)

M T W Th F Sat Sun _____/_____/_____

TODAY I'M GRATEFUL FOR:

_____
_____
_____
_____
_____

MY PRAYER FOR TODAY:

_____
_____
_____
_____
_____

M T W Th F Sat Sun _____ / _____ / _____

TODAY I'M GRATEFUL FOR:

_____
_____
_____
_____

MY PRAYER FOR TODAY:

_____
_____
_____
_____
_____

Delight thyself also in the Lord: and he shall give thee the desires of thine heart. — Psalm 37:4 (KJV)

M T W Th F Sat Sun _____ / _____ / _____

TODAY I'M GRATEFUL FOR:

_____
_____
_____
_____

MY PRAYER FOR TODAY:

_____
_____
_____
_____
_____

M T W Th F Sat Sun _____ / _____ / _____

TODAY I'M GRATEFUL FOR:

_____

_____

_____

_____

MY PRAYER FOR TODAY:

_____

_____

_____

_____

_____

And the Word was made flesh, and dwelt among us, (and we
beheld his glory, the glory as of the only begotten of the Father,)
full of grace and truth. — John 1:14 (KJV)

M T W Th F Sat Sun _____ / _____ / _____

TODAY I'M GRATEFUL FOR:

_____

_____

_____

_____

MY PRAYER FOR TODAY:

_____

_____

_____

_____

_____

M T W Th F Sat Sun _____ / _____ / _____

TODAY I'M GRATEFUL FOR:

MY PRAYER FOR TODAY:

Knowing this, that the trying of your faith worketh patience.
But let patience have her perfect work, that ye may be perfect
and entire, wanting nothing. — James 1:3-4 (KJV)

M T W Th F Sat Sun _____ / _____ / _____

TODAY I'M GRATEFUL FOR:

MY PRAYER FOR TODAY:

M T W Th F Sat Sun _____ / _____ / _____

TODAY I'M GRATEFUL FOR:

MY PRAYER FOR TODAY:

Let us therefore come boldly unto the throne of grace, that we may obtain mercy, and find grace to help in time of need. — Hebrews 4:16 (KJV)

M T W Th F Sat Sun _____ / _____ / _____

TODAY I'M GRATEFUL FOR:

MY PRAYER FOR TODAY:

M T W Th F Sat Sun _____ / _____ / _____

TODAY I'M GRATEFUL FOR:

MY PRAYER FOR TODAY:

Neither is there salvation in any other: for there is none other name under heaven given among men, whereby we must be saved. — Acts 4:12 (KJV)

M T W Th F Sat Sun _____ / _____ / _____

TODAY I'M GRATEFUL FOR:

MY PRAYER FOR TODAY:

M T W Th F Sat Sun _____/_____/_____

TODAY I'M GRATEFUL FOR:

_____
_____
_____
_____

MY PRAYER FOR TODAY:

_____
_____
_____
_____
_____

Thou wilt keep him in perfect peace, whose mind
is stayed on thee: because he trusteth
in thee. — Isaiah 26:3 (KJV)

M T W Th F Sat Sun _____/_____/_____

TODAY I'M GRATEFUL FOR:

_____
_____
_____
_____

MY PRAYER FOR TODAY:

_____
_____
_____
_____

M T W Th F Sat Sun _____ / _____ / _____

TODAY I'M GRATEFUL FOR:

_____
_____
_____
_____

MY PRAYER FOR TODAY:

_____
_____
_____
_____
_____

Lo, I am with you always, even unto the end of the world. — Matthew 28:20 (KJV)

M T W Th F Sat Sun _____ / _____ / _____

TODAY I'M GRATEFUL FOR:

_____
_____
_____
_____

MY PRAYER FOR TODAY:

_____
_____
_____
_____
_____

M T W Th F Sat Sun _____/_____/_____

TODAY I'M GRATEFUL FOR:

_____
_____
_____
_____

MY PRAYER FOR TODAY:

_____
_____
_____
_____
_____

And whatsoever ye do, do it heartily, as to the Lord, and not unto men; Knowing that of the Lord ye shall receive the reward of the inheritance: for ye serve the Lord Christ. — Colossians 3:23-24 (KJV)

M T W Th F Sat Sun _____/_____/_____

TODAY I'M GRATEFUL FOR:

_____
_____
_____
_____

MY PRAYER FOR TODAY:

_____
_____
_____
_____
_____

M T W Th F Sat Sun _____ / _____ / _____

TODAY I'M GRATEFUL FOR:

_____
_____
_____
_____

MY PRAYER FOR TODAY:

_____
_____
_____
_____
_____

Let your light so shine before men, that they may see your good works, and glorify your Father which is in heaven. — Matthew 5:16 (KJV)

M T W Th F Sat Sun _____ / _____ / _____

TODAY I'M GRATEFUL FOR:

_____
_____
_____
_____

MY PRAYER FOR TODAY:

_____
_____
_____
_____
_____

M T W Th F Sat Sun _____/_____/_____

TODAY I'M GRATEFUL FOR:

_____
_____
_____
_____

MY PRAYER FOR TODAY:

_____
_____
_____
_____
_____

For my thoughts are not your thoughts, neither are your ways my ways, saith the Lord. — Isaiah 55:8 (KJV)

M T W Th F Sat Sun _____/_____/_____

TODAY I'M GRATEFUL FOR:

_____
_____
_____
_____

MY PRAYER FOR TODAY:

_____
_____
_____
_____

M T W Th F Sat Sun _____ / _____ / _____

TODAY I'M GRATEFUL FOR:

_____
_____
_____
_____

MY PRAYER FOR TODAY:

_____
_____
_____
_____
_____

The secret things belong unto the Lord our God: but those things which are revealed belong unto us and to our children for ever, that we may do all the words of this law. — Deuteronomy 29:29 (KJV)

M T W Th F Sat Sun _____ / _____ / _____

TODAY I'M GRATEFUL FOR:

_____
_____
_____
_____

MY PRAYER FOR TODAY:

_____
_____
_____
_____
_____

M T W Th F Sat Sun _____ / _____ / _____

TODAY I'M GRATEFUL FOR:

_____
_____
_____
_____
_____

MY PRAYER FOR TODAY:

_____
_____
_____
_____
_____
_____

While we look not at the things which are seen, but at the things which are not seen: for the things which are seen are temporal; but the things which are not seen are eternal. — 2 Corinthians 4:18 (KJV)

M T W Th F Sat Sun _____ / _____ / _____

TODAY I'M GRATEFUL FOR:

_____
_____
_____
_____

MY PRAYER FOR TODAY:

_____
_____
_____
_____
_____

M T W Th F Sat Sun _____ / _____ / _____

TODAY I'M GRATEFUL FOR:

_____
_____
_____
_____

MY PRAYER FOR TODAY:

_____
_____
_____
_____
_____

O taste and see that the Lord is good: blessed is the man that trusteth in him. — Psalm 34:8 (KJV)

M T W Th F Sat Sun _____ / _____ / _____

TODAY I'M GRATEFUL FOR:

_____
_____
_____
_____

MY PRAYER FOR TODAY:

_____
_____
_____
_____
_____

M T W Th F Sat Sun _____/_____/_____

TODAY I'M GRATEFUL FOR:

_____
_____
_____
_____

MY PRAYER FOR TODAY:

_____
_____
_____
_____
_____

No weapon that is formed against thee shall prosper; and every tongue that shall rise against thee in judgment thou shalt condemn. — Isaiah 54:17 (KJV)

M T W Th F Sat Sun _____/_____/_____

TODAY I'M GRATEFUL FOR:

_____
_____
_____
_____

MY PRAYER FOR TODAY:

_____
_____
_____
_____
_____

M T W Th F Sat Sun _____ / _____ / _____

TODAY I'M GRATEFUL FOR:

_____
_____
_____
_____

MY PRAYER FOR TODAY:

_____
_____
_____
_____
_____

**But I am like a green olive tree in the house of God:
I trust in the mercy of God for ever
and ever. — Psalm 52:8 (KJV)**

M T W Th F Sat Sun _____ / _____ / _____

TODAY I'M GRATEFUL FOR:

_____
_____
_____
_____

MY PRAYER FOR TODAY:

_____
_____
_____
_____
_____

M T W Th F Sat Sun _____/_____/_____

TODAY I'M GRATEFUL FOR:

_____
_____
_____
_____

MY PRAYER FOR TODAY:

_____
_____
_____
_____
_____

For I am not ashamed of the gospel of Christ: for it is the power of God unto salvation to every one that believeth; to the Jew first, and also to the Greek. — Romans 1:16 (KJV)

M T W Th F Sat Sun _____/_____/_____

TODAY I'M GRATEFUL FOR:

_____
_____
_____
_____

MY PRAYER FOR TODAY:

_____
_____
_____
_____

M T W Th F Sat Sun _____/_____/_____

TODAY I'M GRATEFUL FOR:

_____
_____
_____
_____

MY PRAYER FOR TODAY:

_____
_____
_____
_____

For the Lord is good; his mercy is everlasting; and his truth endureth to all generations. — Psalm 100:5 (KJV)

M T W Th F Sat Sun _____/_____/_____

TODAY I'M GRATEFUL FOR:

_____
_____
_____
_____

MY PRAYER FOR TODAY:

_____
_____
_____
_____

M T W Th F Sat Sun _____/_____/_____

TODAY I'M GRATEFUL FOR:

_____
_____
_____
_____

MY PRAYER FOR TODAY:

_____
_____
_____
_____
_____

I can do all things through Christ which strengtheneth me. — Philippians 4:13 (KJV)

M T W Th F Sat Sun _____/_____/_____

TODAY I'M GRATEFUL FOR:

_____
_____
_____
_____

MY PRAYER FOR TODAY:

_____
_____
_____
_____
_____

M T W Th F Sat Sun _____/_____/_____

TODAY I'M GRATEFUL FOR:

_____
_____
_____
_____

MY PRAYER FOR TODAY:

_____
_____
_____
_____
_____

But thou, O man of God, flee these things; and follow
after righteousness, godliness, faith, love,
patience, meekness. —1 Timothy 6:11 (KJV)

M T W Th F Sat Sun _____/_____/_____

TODAY I'M GRATEFUL FOR:

_____
_____
_____
_____

MY PRAYER FOR TODAY:

_____
_____
_____
_____
_____

M T W Th F Sat Sun _____/_____/_____

TODAY I'M GRATEFUL FOR:

_____
_____
_____
_____

MY PRAYER FOR TODAY:

_____
_____
_____
_____
_____

Be strong and of a good courage, fear not, nor be afraid of them: for the Lord thy God, he it is that doth go with thee; he will not fail thee, nor forsake thee. — Deuteronomy 31:6 (KJV)

M T W Th F Sat Sun _____/_____/_____

TODAY I'M GRATEFUL FOR:

_____
_____
_____
_____

MY PRAYER FOR TODAY:

_____
_____
_____
_____
_____

M T W Th F Sat Sun _____/_____/_____

TODAY I'M GRATEFUL FOR:

_____
_____
_____
_____

MY PRAYER FOR TODAY:

_____
_____
_____
_____
_____

I will lift up mine eyes unto the hills, from whence cometh
my help. My help cometh from the Lord, which made heaven
and earth. — Psalm 121:1-2 (KJV)

M T W Th F Sat Sun _____/_____/_____

TODAY I'M GRATEFUL FOR:

_____
_____
_____
_____

MY PRAYER FOR TODAY:

_____
_____
_____
_____
_____

M T W Th F Sat Sun _____ / _____ / _____

TODAY I'M GRATEFUL FOR:

_____
_____
_____
_____

MY PRAYER FOR TODAY:

_____
_____
_____
_____
_____

And the light shineth in darkness; and the darkness comprehended it not. — John 1:5 (KJV)

M T W Th F Sat Sun _____ / _____ / _____

TODAY I'M GRATEFUL FOR:

_____
_____
_____
_____

MY PRAYER FOR TODAY:

_____
_____
_____
_____
_____

M T W Th F Sat Sun _____/_____/_____

TODAY I'M GRATEFUL FOR:

_____
_____
_____
_____

MY PRAYER FOR TODAY:

_____
_____
_____
_____
_____

I will be the same until your old age, and I will bear you
up when you turn gray. I have made you, and I will carry you;
I will bear and rescue you. — Isaiah 46:4 (CSB)

M T W Th F Sat Sun _____/_____/_____

TODAY I'M GRATEFUL FOR:

_____
_____
_____
_____

MY PRAYER FOR TODAY:

_____
_____
_____
_____
_____

M T W Th F Sat Sun _____ / _____ / _____

TODAY I'M GRATEFUL FOR:

_____
_____
_____
_____

MY PRAYER FOR TODAY:

_____
_____
_____
_____
_____

The Lord thy God in the midst of thee is mighty; he will save, he will rejoice over thee with joy; he will rest in his love, he will joy over thee with singing. — Zephaniah 3:17 (KJV)

M T W Th F Sat Sun _____ / _____ / _____

TODAY I'M GRATEFUL FOR:

_____
_____
_____
_____

MY PRAYER FOR TODAY:

_____
_____
_____
_____
_____

M T W Th F Sat Sun _____ / _____ / _____

TODAY I'M GRATEFUL FOR:

_____
_____
_____
_____

MY PRAYER FOR TODAY:

_____
_____
_____
_____
_____

> Be careful for nothing; but in every thing by prayer and supplication with thanksgiving let your requests be made known unto God. — Philippians 4:6-7 (KJV)

M T W Th F Sat Sun _____ / _____ / _____

TODAY I'M GRATEFUL FOR:

_____
_____
_____
_____

MY PRAYER FOR TODAY:

_____
_____
_____
_____
_____

M T W Th F Sat Sun _____/_____/_____

TODAY I'M GRATEFUL FOR:

_____
_____
_____
_____

MY PRAYER FOR TODAY:

_____
_____
_____
_____
_____

For we are his workmanship, created in Christ Jesus
unto good works, which God hath before ordained that
we should walk in them. — Ephesians 2:10 (KJV)

M T W Th F Sat Sun _____/_____/_____

TODAY I'M GRATEFUL FOR:

_____
_____
_____
_____

MY PRAYER FOR TODAY:

_____
_____
_____
_____
_____

M T W Th F Sat Sun _____/_____/_____

TODAY I'M GRATEFUL FOR:

_____
_____
_____
_____

MY PRAYER FOR TODAY:

_____
_____
_____
_____
_____

For this day is holy unto our Lord: neither be ye sorry; for the joy of the Lord is your strength. — Nehemiah 8:10 (KJV)

M T W Th F Sat Sun _____/_____/_____

TODAY I'M GRATEFUL FOR:

_____
_____
_____
_____

MY PRAYER FOR TODAY:

_____
_____
_____
_____
_____

M T W Th F Sat Sun _____ / _____ / _____

TODAY I'M GRATEFUL FOR:

_____
_____
_____
_____

MY PRAYER FOR TODAY:

_____
_____
_____
_____
_____

Thine eyes did see my substance, yet being unperfect; and in thy book all my members were written, which in continuance were fashioned, when as yet there was none of them. —Psalm 139:16-17 (KJV)

M T W Th F Sat Sun _____ / _____ / _____

TODAY I'M GRATEFUL FOR:

_____
_____
_____
_____

MY PRAYER FOR TODAY:

_____
_____
_____
_____
_____

M T W Th F Sat Sun _____/_____/_____

TODAY I'M GRATEFUL FOR:

_____
_____
_____
_____

MY PRAYER FOR TODAY:

_____
_____
_____
_____
_____

O taste and see that the Lord is good: blessed is the man that trusteth in him. — Psalm 34:8 (KJV)

M T W Th F Sat Sun _____/_____/_____

TODAY I'M GRATEFUL FOR:

_____
_____
_____
_____

MY PRAYER FOR TODAY:

_____
_____
_____
_____
_____

M T W Th F Sat Sun _____/_____/_____

TODAY I'M GRATEFUL FOR:

_____
_____
_____
_____

MY PRAYER FOR TODAY:

_____
_____
_____
_____

God is my strength and power: and he maketh my way perfect. — 2 Samuel 22:33 (KJV)

M T W Th F Sat Sun _____/_____/_____

TODAY I'M GRATEFUL FOR:

_____
_____
_____
_____

MY PRAYER FOR TODAY:

_____
_____
_____
_____

M T W Th F Sat Sun _____ / _____ / _____

TODAY I'M GRATEFUL FOR:

MY PRAYER FOR TODAY:

For God hath not given us the spirit of fear; but of power,
and of love, and of a sound mind. — 2 Timothy 1:7 (KJV)

M T W Th F Sat Sun _____ / _____ / _____

TODAY I'M GRATEFUL FOR:

MY PRAYER FOR TODAY:

M T W Th F Sat Sun _____/_____/_____

TODAY I'M GRATEFUL FOR:

_____
_____
_____
_____

MY PRAYER FOR TODAY:

_____
_____
_____
_____
_____

He that dwelleth in the secret place of the most High shall abide under the shadow of the Almighty. — Psalm 91:1-2 (KJV)

M T W Th F Sat Sun _____/_____/_____

TODAY I'M GRATEFUL FOR:

_____
_____
_____
_____

MY PRAYER FOR TODAY:

_____
_____
_____
_____
_____

M T W Th F Sat Sun _____ / _____ / _____

TODAY I'M GRATEFUL FOR:

_____
_____
_____
_____

MY PRAYER FOR TODAY:

_____
_____
_____
_____
_____

Call unto me, and I will answer thee, and show
thee great and mighty things, which
thou knowest not. — Jeremiah 33:3 (KJV)

M T W Th F Sat Sun _____ / _____ / _____

TODAY I'M GRATEFUL FOR:

_____
_____
_____
_____

MY PRAYER FOR TODAY:

_____
_____
_____
_____

M T W Th F Sat Sun _____/_____/_____

TODAY I'M GRATEFUL FOR:

_____

_____

_____

_____

MY PRAYER FOR TODAY:

_____

_____

_____

_____

_____

**And my soul shall be joyful in the Lord: it
shall rejoice in his salvation. — Psalm 35:9 (KJV)**

M T W Th F Sat Sun _____/_____/_____

TODAY I'M GRATEFUL FOR:

_____

_____

_____

_____

MY PRAYER FOR TODAY:

_____

_____

_____

_____

_____

M T W Th F Sat Sun _____/_____/_____

TODAY I'M GRATEFUL FOR:

_____
_____
_____
_____

MY PRAYER FOR TODAY:

_____
_____
_____
_____
_____

There is therefore now no condemnation to them which are in Christ Jesus, who walk not after the flesh, but after the Spirit. — Romans 8:1 (KJV)

M T W Th F Sat Sun _____/_____/_____

TODAY I'M GRATEFUL FOR:

_____
_____
_____
_____

MY PRAYER FOR TODAY:

_____
_____
_____
_____
_____

M T W Th F Sat Sun _____/_____/_____

TODAY I'M GRATEFUL FOR:

_____
_____
_____
_____

MY PRAYER FOR TODAY:

_____
_____
_____
_____
_____

Being confident of this very thing, that he which hath begun a good work in you will perform it until the day of Jesus Christ. — Philippians 1:6 (KJV)

M T W Th F Sat Sun _____/_____/_____

TODAY I'M GRATEFUL FOR:

_____
_____
_____
_____

MY PRAYER FOR TODAY:

_____
_____
_____
_____
_____

M T W Th F Sat Sun _____/_____/_____

TODAY I'M GRATEFUL FOR:

_____
_____
_____
_____

MY PRAYER FOR TODAY:

_____
_____
_____
_____
_____

When thou passest through the waters, I will be with thee; and through the rivers, they shall not overflow thee: when thou walkest through the fire, thou shalt not be burned. — Psalm 43:2 (KJV)

M T W Th F Sat Sun _____/_____/_____

TODAY I'M GRATEFUL FOR:

_____
_____
_____
_____

MY PRAYER FOR TODAY:

_____
_____
_____
_____
_____

M T W Th F Sat Sun _____/_____/_____

```
┌─────────────────────────────────────────────┐
│              TODAY I'M GRATEFUL FOR:          │
│  _____  │
│  _____  │
│  _____  │
│  _____  │
└─────────────────────────────────────────────┘
```

```
┌─────────────────────────────────────────────┐
│              MY PRAYER FOR TODAY:             │
│  _____  │
│  _____  │
│  _____  │
│  _____  │
│  _____  │
└─────────────────────────────────────────────┘
```

The righteous cry, and the Lord heareth, and delivereth them out of all their troubles. — Psalm 34:17 (KJV)

M T W Th F Sat Sun _____/_____/_____

```
┌─────────────────────────────────────────────┐
│              TODAY I'M GRATEFUL FOR:          │
│  _____  │
│  _____  │
│  _____  │
│  _____  │
└─────────────────────────────────────────────┘
```

```
┌─────────────────────────────────────────────┐
│              MY PRAYER FOR TODAY:             │
│  _____  │
│  _____  │
│  _____  │
│  _____  │
│  _____  │
└─────────────────────────────────────────────┘
```

M T W Th F Sat Sun _____ / _____ / _____

TODAY I'M GRATEFUL FOR:

_____

_____

_____

_____

MY PRAYER FOR TODAY:

_____

_____

_____

_____

_____

But as it is written, Eye hath not seen, nor ear heard, neither have entered into the heart of man, the things which God hath prepared for them that love him. — 1 Corinthians 2:9 (KJV)

M T W Th F Sat Sun _____ / _____ / _____

TODAY I'M GRATEFUL FOR:

_____

_____

_____

_____

MY PRAYER FOR TODAY:

_____

_____

_____

_____

_____

M T W Th F Sat Sun _____/_____/_____

TODAY I'M GRATEFUL FOR:

_____
_____
_____
_____

MY PRAYER FOR TODAY:

_____
_____
_____
_____
_____

For I am not ashamed of the gospel of Christ: for it is the power of God unto salvation to every one that believeth; to the Jew first, and also to the Greek. — Romans 1:16 (KJV)

M T W Th F Sat Sun _____/_____/_____

TODAY I'M GRATEFUL FOR:

_____
_____
_____
_____

MY PRAYER FOR TODAY:

_____
_____
_____
_____
_____

M T W Th F Sat Sun _____/_____/_____

TODAY I'M GRATEFUL FOR:

_____
_____
_____
_____

MY PRAYER FOR TODAY:

_____
_____
_____
_____
_____

Be still, and know that I am God: I will be
exalted among the heathen, I will be
exalted in the earth. — Psalm 46:10-11 (KJV)

M T W Th F Sat Sun _____/_____/_____

TODAY I'M GRATEFUL FOR:

_____
_____
_____
_____

MY PRAYER FOR TODAY:

_____
_____
_____
_____
_____

M T W Th F Sat Sun _____/_____/_____

TODAY I'M GRATEFUL FOR:

_____
_____
_____
_____

MY PRAYER FOR TODAY:

_____
_____
_____
_____
_____

And it shall come to pass, that whosoever
shall call on the name of the
Lord shall be saved. — Acts 2:21 (KJV)

M T W Th F Sat Sun _____/_____/_____

TODAY I'M GRATEFUL FOR:

_____
_____
_____
_____

MY PRAYER FOR TODAY:

_____
_____
_____
_____
_____

M T W Th F Sat Sun _____ / _____ / _____

TODAY I'M GRATEFUL FOR:

_____
_____
_____
_____
_____

MY PRAYER FOR TODAY:

_____
_____
_____
_____
_____
_____

Yet the Lord will command his lovingkindness in the day time, and in the night his song shall be with me, and my prayer unto the God of my life. — Psalm 42:8 (KJV)

M T W Th F Sat Sun _____ / _____ / _____

TODAY I'M GRATEFUL FOR:

_____
_____
_____
_____
_____

MY PRAYER FOR TODAY:

_____
_____
_____
_____
_____

M T W Th F Sat Sun _____ / _____ / _____

TODAY I'M GRATEFUL FOR:

_____

_____

_____

_____

MY PRAYER FOR TODAY:

_____

_____

_____

_____

_____

The steps of a good man are ordered by the Lord:
and he delighteth in his way. — Psalm 37:23 (KJV)

M T W Th F Sat Sun _____ / _____ / _____

TODAY I'M GRATEFUL FOR:

_____

_____

_____

_____

MY PRAYER FOR TODAY:

_____

_____

_____

_____

_____

M T W Th F Sat Sun _____ / _____ / _____

TODAY I'M GRATEFUL FOR:

_____
_____
_____
_____
_____

MY PRAYER FOR TODAY:

_____
_____
_____
_____
_____

And the Word was made flesh, and dwelt among us, (and we beheld his glory, the glory as of the only begotten of the Father,) full of grace and truth. — John 1:14 (KJV)

M T W Th F Sat Sun _____ / _____ / _____

TODAY I'M GRATEFUL FOR:

_____
_____
_____
_____
_____

MY PRAYER FOR TODAY:

_____
_____
_____
_____
_____

M T W Th F Sat Sun _____ / _____ / _____

TODAY I'M GRATEFUL FOR:

_____
_____
_____
_____

MY PRAYER FOR TODAY:

_____
_____
_____
_____
_____

Every good gift and every perfect gift is from above, and cometh down from the Father of lights, with whom is no variableness, neither shadow of turning. — James 1:17 (KJV)

M T W Th F Sat Sun _____ / _____ / _____

TODAY I'M GRATEFUL FOR:

_____
_____
_____
_____

MY PRAYER FOR TODAY:

_____
_____
_____
_____
_____

M T W Th F Sat Sun _____/_____/_____

TODAY I'M GRATEFUL FOR:

_____
_____
_____
_____
_____

MY PRAYER FOR TODAY:

_____
_____
_____
_____
_____
_____

Therefore I say unto you, What things soever ye
desire, when ye pray, believe that ye receive them,
and ye shall have them. — Mark 11:24 (KJV)

M T W Th F Sat Sun _____/_____/_____

TODAY I'M GRATEFUL FOR:

_____
_____
_____
_____
_____

MY PRAYER FOR TODAY:

_____
_____
_____
_____
_____

M T W Th F Sat Sun _____ / _____ / _____

TODAY I'M GRATEFUL FOR:

_____
_____
_____
_____

MY PRAYER FOR TODAY:

_____
_____
_____
_____
_____

Pray without ceasing. In every thing give thanks:
for this is the will of God in Christ Jesus
concerning you. — 1 Thessalonians 5:17-18 (KJV)

M T W Th F Sat Sun _____ / _____ / _____

TODAY I'M GRATEFUL FOR:

_____
_____
_____
_____

MY PRAYER FOR TODAY:

_____
_____
_____
_____
_____

M T W Th F Sat Sun _____ / _____ / _____

TODAY I'M GRATEFUL FOR:

_____
_____
_____
_____

MY PRAYER FOR TODAY:

_____
_____
_____
_____
_____

**Trust in him at all times; ye people, pour
out your heart before him: God
is a refuge for us. — Psalm 62:8 (KJV)**

M T W Th F Sat Sun _____ / _____ / _____

TODAY I'M GRATEFUL FOR:

_____
_____
_____
_____

MY PRAYER FOR TODAY:

_____
_____
_____
_____
_____

M T W Th F Sat Sun _____ / _____ / _____

TODAY I'M GRATEFUL FOR:

_____
_____
_____
_____

MY PRAYER FOR TODAY:

_____
_____
_____
_____
_____

A friend loveth at all times, and a brother is born for adversity. — Proverbs 17:17 (KJV)

M T W Th F Sat Sun _____ / _____ / _____

TODAY I'M GRATEFUL FOR:

_____
_____
_____
_____

MY PRAYER FOR TODAY:

_____
_____
_____
_____
_____

M T W Th F Sat Sun _____/_____/_____

TODAY I'M GRATEFUL FOR:

_____
_____
_____
_____

MY PRAYER FOR TODAY:

_____
_____
_____
_____
_____

One thing have I desired of the Lord, that will I seek after; that I may dwell in the house of the Lord all the days of my life, to behold the beauty of the Lord, and to enquire in his temple. — Psalm 27:4 (KJV)

M T W Th F Sat Sun _____/_____/_____

TODAY I'M GRATEFUL FOR:

_____
_____
_____
_____

MY PRAYER FOR TODAY:

_____
_____
_____
_____
_____

M T W Th F Sat Sun _____/_____/_____

TODAY I'M GRATEFUL FOR:

_____
_____
_____
_____

MY PRAYER FOR TODAY:

_____
_____
_____
_____
_____

To every thing there is a season, and a time to every purpose under the heaven. — Ecclesiastes 3:1 (KJV)

M T W Th F Sat Sun _____/_____/_____

TODAY I'M GRATEFUL FOR:

_____
_____
_____
_____

MY PRAYER FOR TODAY:

_____
_____
_____
_____
_____

M T W Th F Sat Sun _____ / _____ / _____

TODAY I'M GRATEFUL FOR:

_____
_____
_____
_____

MY PRAYER FOR TODAY:

_____
_____
_____
_____
_____

The Lord is on my side; I will not fear. — Psalm 118:6 (KJV)

M T W Th F Sat Sun _____ / _____ / _____

TODAY I'M GRATEFUL FOR:

_____
_____
_____
_____

MY PRAYER FOR TODAY:

_____
_____
_____
_____

M T W Th F Sat Sun _____ / _____ / _____

TODAY I'M GRATEFUL FOR:

_____
_____
_____
_____

MY PRAYER FOR TODAY:

_____
_____
_____
_____
_____

For with God nothing shall be impossible. — Luke 1:37 (KJV)

M T W Th F Sat Sun _____ / _____ / _____

TODAY I'M GRATEFUL FOR:

_____
_____
_____
_____

MY PRAYER FOR TODAY:

_____
_____
_____
_____
_____

M T W Th F Sat Sun _____ / _____ / _____

TODAY I'M GRATEFUL FOR:

MY PRAYER FOR TODAY:

The grass withereth, the flower fadeth: but the word of our God shall stand for ever. — Isaiah 40:8 (KJV)

M T W Th F Sat Sun _____ / _____ / _____

TODAY I'M GRATEFUL FOR:

MY PRAYER FOR TODAY:

M T W Th F Sat Sun _____/_____/_____

TODAY I'M GRATEFUL FOR:

_____
_____
_____
_____

MY PRAYER FOR TODAY:

_____
_____
_____
_____
_____

The Lord is good, a stronghold in the day of trouble; he knows those who take refuge in him. — Nahum 1:7 (KJV)

M T W Th F Sat Sun _____/_____/_____

TODAY I'M GRATEFUL FOR:

_____
_____
_____
_____

MY PRAYER FOR TODAY:

_____
_____
_____
_____
_____

M T W Th F Sat Sun _____/_____/_____

TODAY I'M GRATEFUL FOR:

_____
_____
_____
_____
_____

MY PRAYER FOR TODAY:

_____
_____
_____
_____
_____
_____

For his anger endureth but a moment; in his favour
is life: weeping may endure for a night, but joy
cometh in the morning. — Psalm 30:5 (KJV)

M T W Th F Sat Sun _____/_____/_____

TODAY I'M GRATEFUL FOR:

_____
_____
_____
_____

MY PRAYER FOR TODAY:

_____
_____
_____
_____
_____

M T W Th F Sat Sun _____ / _____ / _____

TODAY I'M GRATEFUL FOR:

_____

_____

_____

_____

MY PRAYER FOR TODAY:

_____

_____

_____

_____

_____

Now these three remain: faith, hope, and love—but
the greatest of these is love. — 1 Corinthians 13:13 (CSB)

M T W Th F Sat Sun _____ / _____ / _____

TODAY I'M GRATEFUL FOR:

_____

_____

_____

_____

MY PRAYER FOR TODAY:

_____

_____

_____

_____

_____

M T W Th F Sat Sun _____/_____/_____

TODAY I'M GRATEFUL FOR:

_____
_____
_____
_____

MY PRAYER FOR TODAY:

_____
_____
_____
_____
_____

This is the day which the Lord hath made; we will rejoice and be glad in it. — Psalm 118:24 (KJV)

M T W Th F Sat Sun _____/_____/_____

TODAY I'M GRATEFUL FOR:

_____
_____
_____
_____

MY PRAYER FOR TODAY:

_____
_____
_____
_____
_____

M T W Th F Sat Sun _____ / _____ / _____

TODAY I'M GRATEFUL FOR:

_____
_____
_____
_____

MY PRAYER FOR TODAY:

_____
_____
_____
_____
_____

Because thy lovingkindness is better than life, my lips shall praise thee. Thus will I bless thee while I live: I will lift up my hands in thy name. — Psalm 63:3-4 (KJV)

M T W Th F Sat Sun _____ / _____ / _____

TODAY I'M GRATEFUL FOR:

_____
_____
_____
_____

MY PRAYER FOR TODAY:

_____
_____
_____
_____
_____

M T W Th F Sat Sun _____/_____/_____

TODAY I'M GRATEFUL FOR:

_____
_____
_____
_____
_____

MY PRAYER FOR TODAY:

_____
_____
_____
_____
_____
_____

I will both lay me down in peace, and sleep: for thou,
Lord, only makest me dwell in safety. — Psalm 4:8 (KJV)

M T W Th F Sat Sun _____/_____/_____

TODAY I'M GRATEFUL FOR:

_____
_____
_____
_____

MY PRAYER FOR TODAY:

_____
_____
_____
_____
_____

M T W Th F Sat Sun _____ / _____ / _____

TODAY I'M GRATEFUL FOR:

_____

_____

_____

_____

MY PRAYER FOR TODAY:

_____

_____

_____

_____

_____

For thou, Lord, wilt bless the righteous; with favour wilt thou compass him as with a shield. — Psalm 5:12 (KJV)

M T W Th F Sat Sun _____ / _____ / _____

TODAY I'M GRATEFUL FOR:

_____

_____

_____

_____

MY PRAYER FOR TODAY:

_____

_____

_____

_____

_____

M T W Th F Sat Sun _____ / _____ / _____

TODAY I'M GRATEFUL FOR:

_____
_____
_____
_____

MY PRAYER FOR TODAY:

_____
_____
_____
_____
_____

The Lord hath heard my supplication; the
Lord will receive my prayer. — Psalm 6:9 (KJV)

M T W Th F Sat Sun _____ / _____ / _____

TODAY I'M GRATEFUL FOR:

_____
_____
_____
_____

MY PRAYER FOR TODAY:

_____
_____
_____
_____
_____

M T W Th F Sat Sun _____ / _____ / _____

TODAY I'M GRATEFUL FOR:

_____
_____
_____
_____

MY PRAYER FOR TODAY:

_____
_____
_____
_____
_____

O Lord, our Lord, how excellent is thy name in all the earth!
who hast set thy glory above the heavens. — Psalm 8:8 (KJV)

M T W Th F Sat Sun _____ / _____ / _____

TODAY I'M GRATEFUL FOR:

_____
_____
_____
_____

MY PRAYER FOR TODAY:

_____
_____
_____
_____
_____

M T W Th F Sat Sun _____ / _____ / _____

TODAY I'M GRATEFUL FOR:

MY PRAYER FOR TODAY:

He will cover you with his feathers; you will take refuge under his wings. His faithfulness will be a protective shield. — Psalm 91:4 (CSB)

M T W Th F Sat Sun _____ / _____ / _____

TODAY I'M GRATEFUL FOR:

MY PRAYER FOR TODAY:

M T W Th F Sat Sun _____/_____/_____

TODAY I'M GRATEFUL FOR:

_____
_____
_____
_____

MY PRAYER FOR TODAY:

_____
_____
_____
_____
_____

> But it is good for me to draw near to God: I have
> put my trust in the Lord God, that I may
> declare all thy works. — Psalm 73:28 (KJV)

M T W Th F Sat Sun _____/_____/_____

TODAY I'M GRATEFUL FOR:

_____
_____
_____
_____

MY PRAYER FOR TODAY:

_____
_____
_____
_____
_____

M T W Th F Sat Sun _____/_____/_____

TODAY I'M GRATEFUL FOR:

_____
_____
_____
_____

MY PRAYER FOR TODAY:

_____
_____
_____
_____
_____
_____

Therefore the Lord is waiting to show you mercy, and is rising up
to show you compassion, for the Lord is a just God. All who
wait patiently for him are happy. — Isaiah 30:18 (CSB)

M T W Th F Sat Sun _____/_____/_____

TODAY I'M GRATEFUL FOR:

_____
_____
_____
_____

MY PRAYER FOR TODAY:

_____
_____
_____
_____
_____

M T W Th F Sat Sun _____/_____/_____

TODAY I'M GRATEFUL FOR:

_____
_____
_____
_____

MY PRAYER FOR TODAY:

_____
_____
_____
_____
_____

He said: Lord God of Israel, there is no God like you in heaven above or on earth below, who keeps the gracious covenant with your servants who walk before you with all their heart. — 1 Kings 8:23 (CSB)

M T W Th F Sat Sun _____/_____/_____

TODAY I'M GRATEFUL FOR:

_____
_____
_____
_____

MY PRAYER FOR TODAY:

_____
_____
_____
_____
_____

M T W Th F Sat Sun _____/_____/_____

TODAY I'M GRATEFUL FOR:

_____
_____
_____
_____

MY PRAYER FOR TODAY:

_____
_____
_____
_____
_____

Submit yourselves therefore to God. Resist the devil, and he will flee from you. — James 4:7 (KJV)

M T W Th F Sat Sun _____/_____/_____

TODAY I'M GRATEFUL FOR:

_____
_____
_____
_____

MY PRAYER FOR TODAY:

_____
_____
_____
_____
_____

M T W Th F Sat Sun _____ / _____ / _____

TODAY I'M GRATEFUL FOR:

_____

_____

_____

_____

MY PRAYER FOR TODAY:

_____

_____

_____

_____

_____

> Behold, God is my salvation; I will trust, and not be afraid:
> for the Lord Jehovah is my strength and my song; he also
> is become my salvation. — Isaiah 12:2 (KJV)

M T W Th F Sat Sun _____ / _____ / _____

TODAY I'M GRATEFUL FOR:

_____

_____

_____

_____

MY PRAYER FOR TODAY:

_____

_____

_____

_____

_____

M T W Th F Sat Sun _____ / _____ / _____

TODAY I'M GRATEFUL FOR:

_____
_____
_____
_____
_____

MY PRAYER FOR TODAY:

_____
_____
_____
_____
_____
_____

Enter into his gates with thanksgiving, and into his courts with praise: be thankful unto him, and bless his name. — Psalm 100:4 (KJV)

M T W Th F Sat Sun _____ / _____ / _____

TODAY I'M GRATEFUL FOR:

_____
_____
_____
_____

MY PRAYER FOR TODAY:

_____
_____
_____
_____
_____

M T W Th F Sat Sun _____ / _____ / _____

TODAY I'M GRATEFUL FOR:

_____
_____
_____
_____

MY PRAYER FOR TODAY:

_____
_____
_____
_____
_____

Ask, and it shall be given you; seek, and ye shall find; knock, and it shall be opened unto you. — Matthew 7: 7 (KJV)

M T W Th F Sat Sun _____ / _____ / _____

TODAY I'M GRATEFUL FOR:

_____
_____
_____
_____

MY PRAYER FOR TODAY:

_____
_____
_____
_____
_____

M T W Th F Sat Sun _____ / _____ / _____

TODAY I'M GRATEFUL FOR:

_____
_____
_____
_____

MY PRAYER FOR TODAY:

_____
_____
_____
_____
_____

... but as for me and my house, we will
serve the Lord. — Joshua 24:15b (KJV)

M T W Th F Sat Sun _____ / _____ / _____

TODAY I'M GRATEFUL FOR:

_____
_____
_____
_____

MY PRAYER FOR TODAY:

_____
_____
_____
_____

M T W Th F Sat Sun _____/_____/_____

TODAY I'M GRATEFUL FOR:

_____
_____
_____
_____

MY PRAYER FOR TODAY:

_____
_____
_____
_____
_____

Blessed is the man that trusteth in the Lord, and
whose hope the Lord is. — Jeremiah 17:7 (KJV)

M T W Th F Sat Sun _____/_____/_____

TODAY I'M GRATEFUL FOR:

_____
_____
_____
_____

MY PRAYER FOR TODAY:

_____
_____
_____
_____
_____

M T W Th F Sat Sun _____ / _____ / _____

TODAY I'M GRATEFUL FOR:

_____
_____
_____
_____

MY PRAYER FOR TODAY:

_____
_____
_____
_____
_____

O give thanks unto the Lord, for he is good:
for his mercy endureth for ever. — Psalm 107:1 (KJV)

M T W Th F Sat Sun _____ / _____ / _____

TODAY I'M GRATEFUL FOR:

_____
_____
_____
_____

MY PRAYER FOR TODAY:

_____
_____
_____
_____
_____

Made in the USA
San Bernardino, CA
26 March 2020